DEDICATION

To my mother Jenny Panebianco, you taught me so many things, but above all, you taught me to do the right thing even when no one is watching.

I0480210

CONTENTS

How To Double Conversion Rates

Lessons Learnt Spending Over Five Million Dollars on A/B Split Tests.

By Josh Panebianco

Josh Panebianco

ISBN: 9781799274025

INTRODUCTION

HOW I MADE MY FIRST $1,000 ONLINE

How I made my first $1,000 online started without any grand dreams of creating a million-dollar online business or of working from my laptop while I travelled around the world. Instead, it started while I was a personal trainer. A few years out of high school, I had started my own business and had one main goal: to find more clients in order to grow my business.

When I first started as a personal trainer, I thought being successful meant helping people get in shape and keeping them accountable. While that was why clients kept coming back, the hardest part was actually finding new clients in the first place. I quickly learnt that what really makes you a successful personal trainer is your ability to market yourself and find new clients. This really hit home for me when I discovered that the most popular personal trainer in my area was an out-of-shape 40-something guy with grey hair. Don't get me wrong – he was a very nice guy and clearly was very good at his job, but he was definitely not who you would expect to be the #1 personal trainer in the area.

The truth is that being a personal trainer is like being a salesman. You can't make any money unless you invest in your own marketing in order to drive new leads, and drive new business. Take this for example – the average lifespan of a new personal trainer is less than 18 months. New trainers spend thousands of dollars to get certified only to discover that personal training has nothing to do with fitness and everything to do with sales and marketing.

During the same time I was discovering the realities

of personal training, my own business was busy but definitely not booked out. I was comfortable, which looking back is one of the most dangerous places to be. In my experience, most people only take action when the pain of staying where they are is greater than the pain of making a change.

At the time, I had no idea about marketing or building websites. In fact, I found the whole idea of marketing very confusing and the thought of writing code downright scary. Fortunately for me, one of my clients at the time was a brilliant digital marketer by the name of Fred Schebesta. Fred was the co-founder of finder.com.au, a very successful credit card comparison website based in Australia. Today, Finder compares virtually everything from cryptocurrency exchanges to electronics and attracts over 4 million visits per month. Fred would go on to build a global company servicing millions of people all around the world.

One night, we went out to dinner after a training session. As we began to chat about our businesses,

Fred explained to me the importance of creating a website that generated leads for new personal training clients. I was quickly sold on the idea of having a steady stream of new clients. The only thing standing in my way was learning how to build a website.

Following Fred's advice, I bought a domain and hosting and put together one of the ugliest and most unprofessional looking websites anyone has ever seen. To be clear, I was not proud of this website at first – it was *definitely not* going to win any design awards. However, simply creating a functional live website taught me two extremely valuable lessons that still guide my decisions today.

Firstly, learn from someone who has already accomplished your goal. Whether that requires signing up for an online class or even paying for his or her time, it is almost always worth it. The key principle is to focus on not what they say, but rather what they do. This can instantly shave massive amounts of time and money from the early trial-

and-error phase of starting a new business.

Secondly, it taught me to focus on progress, not perfection. The first step to getting ahead is to get started. While my first website was ugly and buggy, it was up and running. This meant that I had something to build on. The main reason why getting *something* out into the world is better than waiting until it's perfect is that you have the opportunity to get real feedback from your target audience.

Waiting for perfection leads to what's called a false positive. When you show your close friends and family, they almost always give you positive feedback because they don't want to hurt your feelings. As a result, you get a misconception about how great your website is even though you have not sold a single thing.

Nothing happens until something is sold.

Stop listening to people that have not and will not buy your product. Their two cents is worth exactly that. Ask complete strangers to buy your product.

Then and only then will you know if you have a winner or not.

Much of the reason I am the marketer I am today is because of early lessons that Fred taught me. I am very grateful to him for that. With Fred's help and countless hours of banging my head against the wall, I finally built a website that allowed a user to fill out a form with his or her contact details. This may sound overly simple, but at the time, I was thrilled that I had a functioning website that could generate new leads for my business. What I then discovered was that to get a site up and running was really just the first step. The next step is driving traffic to the site in order to convert leads into new customers. This led me to my next learning experience.

Traffic is easy. Customers are not.

When most people start measuring web traffic, they typically pick an arbitrary number out of thin air. The key thing to remember is that you don't want traffic. You want commercial intent. That means you want people who want what you have to sell.

How did I generate traffic with people that wanted personal training without a big marketing budget or frankly, any marketing budget at all? The answer is simple – I created content or rather articles, to be specific. I wrote on a variety of topics related to fitness and health. Very slowly but surely, I started building traffic to my personal training website. The key word in the process is "slow". I wrote one article per week for at least six months before I started seeing any real traffic. Keep in mind, this was the very early days of search engine marketing, a time when digital marketing was in its infancy. I was fortunate enough to have a mentor show me the way.

The goal of the site was lead generation. The site was just an offer and a form to fill out if you were interested. The offer was simple – receive a free personal training session in exchange for your contact details.

After a few months, I started seeing people fill out the form, but sadly most of the time, it was spam or other personal trainers trying to sell me stuff. During this time I wanted to give up; the only thing keeping me going was that I was steadily climbing the search results pages for personal-trainer-related keywords. I knew that if that continued I would soon be on the first page for people searching for personal training in my area.

It was at least six to eight months of creating content, I finally reached the first page for personal training keywords. After that, I started seeing not spammers or other trainers, but real prospects fill out the form. I met my first prospect in person and gave them a free personal training session. Right after the session, they signed up to train with me three days per week for a total of $960 a month. Later that same week, I had another person sign up via the website. This time it was only once a week for a total of $320 a month. Within one week, I increased my monthly income by $1280.

That's how I made my first $1,000 online.

The rest was history. The following weeks, people were constantly visiting and filling out the form on my website. I began generating so many leads that I started having other personal trainers reach out to me to either partner with me or buy leads off me that I could not use. Turns out the leads almost always converted into clients for other trainers as well.

Following the success of my first website, I built up confidence to create a second site, this time selling fitness products.

Again, I went to Fred for advice. He suggested that I focus on the following – sell just one product online and make at least one dollar of profit. If you can make a one-dollar profit, then you can make a million-dollar profit. The idea of taking one step at a time towards building something bigger still guides my decisions today.

I decided to sell a product that I used myself – Swiss Balls. They were also very cheap to buy and easy to ship to customers. I followed the same process that I did for my personal training website: create content related to the product for six to eight months. Given my previous experience, I reached the first page of search results in a little over four months. Shortly afterwards, I sold my first Swiss Ball for a total profit of $27.

I had done it. I had made at least a one-dollar profit from selling something on the internet. I was no longer thinking about personal training. I was obsessed with selling products online. The Swiss Ball website grew each and every month until I had a very predictable and steady source of income to supplement my personal training business.

This is when I realized that I was now a much better digital marketer than I was a personal trainer. Shortly after deciding to focus on digital marketing full-time, I slowly transitioned out of personal training. To be honest, it was hard to say goodbye to some of my clients, but I knew that I needed to make a change. I then started to do freelance work for other businesses in the fitness industry and, later expanded to other industries, such as financial services.

Ten years later, I'm still doing what I love, and the businesses I work with are thrilled with my results. I have managed multi-million dollar advertising campaigns in the most competitive industries in the United States. I have more than doubled conversion rates for these companies and have become an expert in conversion rate optimization.

This book is the result of the last ten years of real-world marketing strategies that have consistently doubled conversion rates for my clients. I hope the secrets in this book dramatically increase the conversion rates for your advertising campaigns.

HOW TO TURN ADVERTISING DOLLARS INTO PROFIT

The first goal of this book is to help you turn the money you spend on advertising into profit. That sounds simple enough but don't mistake simple for easy. I have spent the last ten years of my life selling products and services online, and only through massive amounts of trial and error have I been able to establish concrete rules on what truly works and what doesn't. The good news is, you don't have to make the same mistakes I did, and, best of all, you don't have to spend ten years making them.

The second goal of this book is to turn over ten years of marketing experience into something that you could read in only a few days. Turning decades into days has been something that has always fascinated me. An author can spend 40 years learning and researching everything there is to know about a certain topic, only to publish their findings in a book that anyone can buy for next to nothing and read in under a week.This is the power of learning from other people's mistakes instead of your own. Learn from my mistakes — your wallet will thank you for it.

My aim is for this book to be slender but juicy– no fluff nor filler, only battle-tested marketing strategies that have repeatedly turned advertising dollars into profit. If you are reading this book, the chances are you've spent money on advertising and have not made a profit. You are not alone. The vast majority of business owners achieve negative or at best, breakeven results with the money they spend on advertising. Why is this so? In my experience, they make three critical mistakes.

Firstly, they have a complete lack of any marketing intelligence. What I mean by marketing intelligence is that they have no clear framework on what makes effective advertising. They simply copy other ads that they like. As a result, they copy other people's mistakes, but they do an even worse job than the first person. That's because they have no clear guidelines on how to critically analyze a piece of advertising. In this book, you will learn a simple, easy-to-understand set of rules and principles that you can instantly use to evaluate marketing in a way that quickly tells which ads are winners and which ads are going to send you broke.

Secondly, they either don't measure the right things or, even worse, they don't measure anything at all. The performance of an athlete increases when that athlete starts to measure his or her performance. Marketing is no different. Marketing is a numbers game. Warren Buffett once said, "if you can't read the scoreboard. You don't know the score. If you don't know the score, you can't tell the winners from the losers." This book will teach you how to create your own marketing scoreboard, so you can know at all times if you are winning or losing.

Lastly, they don't use a scientific testing framework to accurately determine the results of their marketing campaigns. They make changes because they like how it looks or because one person said they don't like it. Individual opinions are cheap, Data is what is truly valuable. This book will help you make data-driven marketing decisions that will create a predictable increase in the conversion rates of your marketing campaigns.

THE ONE THING THAT IS NOT GOING ANYWHERE

Technology is changing so fast that it's nearly impossible to keep up with everything that is going on. Marketing has always been at the bleeding edge of this race for a better, faster tomorrow.

This tidal wave of change and innovation can easily become overwhelming. Questions come up in your mind, like:

- What type of content should I create?
- Should I start a blog or a podcast?
- What is the best type of camera to use when making videos?
- Should I learn to code?

- Do I need to go back to school to learn how to sell things online?
- Do I need to pay for expensive marketing automation software?
- Should I learn to build my own website, or should I hire a web developer?
- Which social media platform should I invest time in?

These are all important questions worth answering. When you sit down and think about it, all of these questions are really asking the same thing: what will return the greatest result for me and my business? If you had to master one thing, what would that be?

My advice to you is this: focus on the one thing that is not going away. This one thing, when mastered, will create more money for you than you ever thought possible.

So, what is the one thing that is not going anywhere?

Learning how to turn advertising into profit.

The exchange of attention for money is the one thing that is not going anywhere. Smartphones are going to change. The internet is going to change. The way we consume content has changed more in the last ten years than in the last 200 years.

But regardless of what happens with technology, companies and individuals that own or have access to large audiences of people are going to sell that exposure to other companies for money.

The sooner you realize that your ability to create a positive return on your investment is the single most valuable skill you can master, the better. Then, and only then, will you know that you are secure in your financial future.

THE THREE FACTORS THAT CONTROL CONVERSION RATES

Increasing conversion rates starts with understanding what factors influence conversion rates in the first place. Conversion rates are influenced by three main factors:

1) Marketing
2) Design
3) Technology

I know what you are thinking. Josh, that sounds like a lot to wrap my head around. All I want to see is a return on the money I spend on advertising. I don't have time to learn three different skill sets. But, you don't need to become an expert on all three of these factors. All you need is a working understanding of each factor and how it influences conversion rates.

Marketing

You will never be able to increase conversion rates until you increase your marketing intelligence. If I put ten different ads in front of you, would you be able to tell me which one performed the best without seeing the results? Do you understand the one thing that in the first three seconds will instantly kill the chances of making a sale? Chances are you do not. Increasing your marketing results starts with increasing your understanding of what makes effective marketing in the first place. When you understand the core underlying principles of how to influence someone, you will be in a position of great power.

Design

How you design your marketing material has a massive impact on the performance of your ads.

People buy with their eyes. The last thing you want to do is turn people off before you even get a chance to tell them about your product.

Don't be the fool that turns up to a black tie event in a t-shirt and jeans. Understand your market. The design of your marketing speaks before you even open your mouth. By reading this book, you will able to create a great first impression.

Technology

This is the last thing people should focus on, but sadly technology, is all people want to talk about. Technology enables the marketing message. Not the other way round.

Technology influences conversion rates in three main areas. Firstly, qualification. Technology enables you to preselect who sees your advertising. Secondly, automation — being able to deliver marketing messages to people at scale, something that would previously have been done manually. Lastly, and most importantly, technology enables you to measure the results of your advertising with extreme detail and accuracy.

One important thing to note is that when people think of technology, they automatically think that you need to spend big money on the latest, most expensive marketing software. This could not be further from the truth. All of the tools I use to manage multi-million dollar advertising campaigns can be found for free or, worst case scenario, at very little cost.

This book is broken up into three sections: marketing, design, and technology. After reading all three sections, you will be able to increase conversion rates like you never thought possible.

Now let's get started.

Part One: Marketing

THE SINGLE BIGGEST MARKETING MISTAKE

People ask me all the time what is the one single thing they can do that will dramatically increase their marketing results, that silver bullet that all great marketers carry around in their back pocket. For the record, I don't like this question or other questions similar to this. Winners don't ask this question. It is never one thing. It is always ten things. It's like asking for the postcode instead of the street address.

Even after everything I just told you, I know you still want the answer anyway. The good news is that I have had this question asked of me enough times now that I would have to be a fool not to see the patterns.

The single biggest marketing mistake I see people make is this:

People make marketing material that is creative and subjective instead of measurable and effective.

They make the mistake of creating ads with the goal of building a brand instead of driving sales. They worship at the altar of branding and creative expression. They use fluffy buzzwords like "synergy" and "brand awareness". They focus all their energy on creating a cool brand with a logo they are very proud of. They create marketing campaigns with the goal of making the audience feel a certain way. This is why most people go broke when they spend money on marketing.

The goal of marketing is to influence someone to take action. Marketing is only effective when it can be measured. Measurable marketing is what's known in the advertising world as "direct response advertising". Direct response is about giving someone an offer that compels them to take action. Direct response is about making data-driven decisions instead of just going with your gut.

On the other hand, you have branding. Look, don't get me wrong. There is a time and a place to work on branding, but it should never be the core focus of your advertising campaign. Branding is about what customers say about you after they have bought your product. Branding is very much like your reputation: it's what people say about you when you're not in the room.

The main problem with branding is that it's often not measurable. When marketing companies say they focus on brand awareness, all that really means is that they don't want to be measured and don't want to be held accountable. They can take creative risks with someone else's money. Then, when it fails to bring in any increase in sales, all they have to say is, "well, it did increase brand awareness". Brand awareness will not pay your rent this month.

Only sales will do that.

This is why there is a growing divide in the marketing world between measurable direct response advertising and branding. Anyone that tells you that marketing should not be measurable is either trying to rob you or should be fitted for a straightjacket.

The goal of marketing is to increase sales. Measure everything and know to the dollar the results of each part of your marketing pipeline. This is how you turn marketing dollars into profit. Everything else is gambling.

If you want to see an example of when branding takes over a campaign, look at the car industry. Almost every car ad is exactly the same, and not in a good way. Even the most common and basic cars are marketed as "unlocking a wild beast" or "conquering the mountain" when the truth is that these cars will spend most of their lives sitting in traffic. If you were to sum up car ads in one word, it would be *ignorable*. Don't make the mistake that car companies make. They aim to be witty, funny, or creative. Instead, the aim should always be to influence someone to take action.

This leads us to the first key takeaway from this book.

Key Takeaway #1

Your marketing should aim to be persuasive, not creative.

THE LIE THAT KEEPS YOU BROKE

The most toxic and limiting belief I hear from people whose businesses are not where they want them to be is this: marketing is not as important as the product. If you make a great product the marketing will take care of itself.

No, hell no. This lie is why so many people spend money on a new business idea and fail. Let me make this crystal clear. This very fact might you rethink every business decision you ever make moving forward:

The quality of your marketing is more important than the quality of your product.

If I had the option to invest in a company with an amazing product but terrible marketing or a company with an ordinary product but world-class marketing, I would choose the company with an ordinary product but world-class marketing every single time. The product matters to the extent that it does what you say it does and solves the customer's problem. Everything else falls on the shoulders of marketing.

Apple did not invent the mp3 player, but they did market the mp3 player better than anyone else. *But Josh, the iPod was a great product to start with.* Yes, they took a great product and marketed better than anyone else had before, and that two-punch combo is why they grew to become a trillion-dollar company. The success of the iPod was due to the best marketing the tech industry and ever seen. While other mp3 players offered similar features, the iPod offered you something truly magical. Ten thousand songs in your pocket. Now, who doesn't want that?

The vast majority of people don't want excellence from a service provider, they just want competency. The good news is that the bar is low, very very low. All you need is to be able to solve the customer's problem. Now, I'm not saying you should aim low with the quality of your product. What I am saying is that the quality of the product is secondary to the quality of the marketing.

Chances are, whatever your product or service is, it can help someone solve a problem. With that out of the way all you need now is more of other people's problems to solve. That is not done by making your product or service better, that is achieved by only one thing: marketing.

Great products are more common than you think. How many times have you walked past a great musician standing on a street corner playing just for tips? How many times have you had a great meal in an empty restaurant? Great products are everywhere. Are the most popular musicians in the world also the most talented? A very small group of recording artists rely on pure talent alone, maybe a handful every decade. The rest are good looking people with a decent voice that have been picked up by savvy marketing minds.

Don't believe me? The two most popular music groups during the 90s and early 2000s were both created by the exact same person. This person created the best-selling boy band of all time. Over 130 million records sold. The two groups he created were the Backstreet Boys and NSYNC.

The formula was simple. Take five young men that are all good looking but in five different ways. The tough guy, the baby-faced one, and the one that wears glasses — you know the score. Then, get them to sing very simple songs with catchy hooks about first love and about how every girl will find true love. Then tour high schools, anywhere that teenage girls can see them. Take good looks, formulaic love songs, and a targeted marketing campaign, and boom. You are on to a winner. The highest selling music group of the 90s and 2000s did not make the best music or even have the most talented musicians. What they did have was world-class marketing, and in the end, that is what makes all the difference.

Some of the most successful companies in the world make very ordinary products. In fact, they make products that are downright bad. How does that pizza you had while travelling in Italy compare to the one you ordered last Friday night at 9 p.m.?

By now you are probably thinking, but Josh, it shouldn't be this way. This is not fair. I have a better product than my competition. That should be all that matters. Sorry to tell you, but successful marketing is not about what should be. It's about what is true.

Key Takeaway #2

The quality of your marketing is more important than the quality of your product.

THE UNFAIR ADVANTAGE

In the fifth century BC, China was gripped by a brutal and bloody civil war. During this time, a military commander, strategist, and philosopher emerged. This military commander would go on to create what is widely considered the most important strategic book ever written. A book that continues to influence the minds of military commanders and world leaders to this day. This book is one of only a handful of books in human history that is still widely read and universally praised some 2500 years after it was written.

The name of the military commander was Sun Tzu, and the book he wrote is called *The Art of War*. This book contains only thirteen chapters, each one detailing a strategic military principle that can easily be applied to any part of life. Part of the reason why *The Art of War* is still read to this day is that the principles can be applied to any competitive endeavor, business, sport and, yes, even marketing.

I highly recommend that you read the entire book, but the principle that has the most direct impact on marketing is chapter three, which is a discussion on when and where to attack the enemy. The key quote from this chapter is this:

"If you know the enemy and know yourself, you need not fear the result of a hundred battles. If you know yourself but not the enemy, for every victory gained you will also suffer a defeat. If you know neither the enemy nor yourself, you will succumb in every battle."

— Sun Tzu, The Art of War

Sun Tzu understood the importance of knowing who you are dealing with and how this information can be used to your advantage. Part of the reason Sun Tzu was so successful is that he was willing to dedicate time to research.

Detailed knowledge about who you are dealing with is the unfair advantage. A lack of knowledge and insight will always put you in a position of weakness.

Nothing — and I mean nothing — can replace knowing your customer.

Customer research is the only true advantage that is available to anyone that is willing to do the work.

I know what you are thinking: I already know my customer, I don't need to do any more research. Let me tell you one this for certain: if you are selling less than you would like to, you don't know your customer.

There is a reason why the best quarterbacks in the world spend more time watching a recording of their opponent's games than they do throwing footballs. They know the edge is found in clearly identifying the strengths and weaknesses of their opponent. Don't be the fool that sets foot on the field without doing their homework.

The good news is that when it comes to marketing there are only two main questions we are looking to answer when gathering information about the customer.

1. Who is this person? Define the age, gender, income level, location, and any other specific information about who the customer is.

2. What does this person want? What are the fears and desires of this person? What problem are they looking to solve? What experiences are they looking for?

When you clearly know who your customer is and

what they truly want, then, and only then, will you be able to maximize the results of your marketing campaigns.

In my experience, the only way to gain a true advantage over your competition from the outset is to know more about the customer than they do.

He who knows the customer best wins.

The other key benefit of doing the research about your customer is that it takes the focus away from you and directs energy towards the people you are trying to help.

Sometimes we fall in love with our product when we really should be falling in love with our customers.

Everyone is looking for an edge. You just found one. Know your customer better than your competition. This is the unfair advantage.

So how do you start to get to know your customers better? Personally contact them, make them feel special, make them feel that you care. Don't spam them with an email asking for them complete a survey for nothing in return. Send them something of value. Create an incentive for people to talk with you. Respect your customers' time and compensate them for their valuable feedback.

Take a sample from your customer database. Look to speak with three types of customers. Customers that love your product, customers that used your product only once and never again, and customers that for some reason do not like your product. All three of these customers have something of value to share with you. Take the time to listen the feedback, both positive and negative. You will be glad that you did.

Key Takeaway #3

If you are selling less than you would like to, you don't know your customer.

THE NAPOLEON RULE

Napoleon Bonaparte changed the course of history in more ways than most people will ever realize. Historians debate many aspects of Napoleon's life, but there is one thing that they all agree on. Napoleon was one of the greatest strategic minds that ever lived. His stunning military victories during his rise to power, from being virtually unknown to becoming the Emperor of France, are legendary. To this day, the details of his wartime strategies and battlefield tactics are studied and picked apart by the world's leaders.

History will always remember Napoleon as a master of warfare, but there is one another form of combat that he was a master of like no other. The war of influence.

Napoleon understood the human mind. He understood what motivates someone to take action and what compels them to stand still or even surrender. Napoleon conquered nations with the might of his army, but he also won over the minds of the people of France with his mastery of propaganda. This leads us to the origin of the Napoleon rule.

Napoleon understood the importance of public opinion, especially during times of war. In fact, one of Napoleon's greatest victories was not won on the battlefield but in the minds of the people of France. During his 14 years of government, during which only 14 months were not spent at war, Napoleon received little to no public outcry. Manipulating public opinion on a national scale and for over 14 years would be unheard of in today's age. So how did he achieve this?

Napoleon created entire departments for which the sole purpose was to release military reports and literature that supported Napoleon's political and military agenda. He created his own newspapers, art galleries, and public works in his name — all with a goal to carefully manipulate what the people of France thought of him.

To achieve such a great feat of widespread manipulation, he needed to define what really influences the human mind. What would make a person take action in almost every situation? What could he truly count on in a time of crisis?

"Men are moved by two levers only, fear and self interest."
— Napoleon Bonaparte

Fear and self-interest drive almost all decisions we make, whether we like it or not. This is the Napoleon rule.

Humans are not as sophisticated as we like to think. We may live indoors and carry computers in our pockets, but we will always have one foot in the jungle. Humans are primal emotional creatures. No matter how much we have now, we always want more: more money, more status, and more power. We also have a deep desire to feel safe. Fear and self-interest is what will influence someone to take action in almost every situation.

The key thing to focus on as marketers is this idea of self-interest. The biggest mistake I see people make when talking to people about their product or service is that they talk about themselves, such as which school they went to, how many years of experience they have, the last time they were featured in the newspaper. This is a massive mistake.

The average person does not care about you or your product. They only care about what you can do for them.

Simply changing the conversation from how good you are to how you can specifically and measurably help someone will result in a dramatic increase in response rates from your advertising efforts.

So you got featured in *The New York Times* last year. Great! How does that help me? How does that get me closer to where I want to be? While getting major media outlets to feature you is a great way to build your brand (and it will make your mum very proud of you), never forget the only person that truly cares about that is you (and maybe your mum).

Using other already-established brands to build your own brand by association is what marketers like to call "social proof", which is great for greasing the wheels of conversion after you have demonstrated value, but first, we must make them an offer that gives them something of value.

You are never the offer. The end result of what you can do for them is the offer.

Change the conversation from how good you think you are to what you can offer right now that can help people. Think to yourself, how can you feed the prospect's hunger for more than they have now?

On a personal level, most people don't like the company of people that only speak about themselves. It tells the world that you are insecure, you need to be validated with attention, and you are trying to make up for a personal deficit. On the other hand, most people enjoy it when someone takes a genuine interest in them by relating to them and asking questions that tell the other person that you are listening and that you care. Take this as a sign to take a greater interest in your customer's problems than your own personal achievements.

The second part of the Napoleon rule is fear. Now, using fear to influence people can leave a bad taste in some people's mouths. Remember, humans still have one foot in the jungle, and fear is one of the most powerful primal emotions. To not acknowledge and understand how fear is used to influence people is doing yourself a massive disservice.

The important thing to remember is that great marketers understand that the principles that influence people can be used for either good or evil. A knife can be a weapon, or it could help you make dinner — it all comes down to what you intend to use it for.

One important thing to remember is that people will do much more to avoid pain than they ever will to gain pleasure. The fear of loss, the fear for personal safety being put at risk. Fear plays a bigger part in the decision-making process than most people like to admit.

Aristotle once said:
"The aim of the wise is not to secure pleasure, but to avoid pain."
— Aristotle

With that said, some of the biggest industries in the

world that carry some of the most respected brands base their entire marketing campaigns around selling with fear. The best example of this would be the insurance industry. You don't buy insurance because you like the policy or the salesperson that sold it to you. You buy insurance because it gives you peace of mind and helps you sleep at night.

So how do we use fear to influence people in an ethical and moral way? Simply ask yourself, what is the cost to the person that does not use your product or service? What do they stand to lose? If you spoke to them 12 months from when they didn't take action and buy your product or service, what would you find they have they missed out on? Don't exaggerate here. Be real. Be genuine. Be honest.

Help people avoid unnecessary pain or loss by giving them something of value that helps them to avoid pain. A simple way to do this is to this is to remind people that sometimes the most costly action is inaction. What is the cost of waiting until next week or even next year? This is an ethical and moral way to influence with fear.

Here is a takeaway that is easy to remember:

Key Takeaway #4

If you find the prospect's pain you will find their wallet.

The Napoleon rule is so powerful because it takes advantage of two fundamental human traits in one fell swoop. It's the marketing two-punch combination that will leave even savvy veteran marketers helpless to resist it.

Good marketers use the first part of the Napoleon rule to influence their audience to take action. Great marketers use both. Never create another advertisement again without at least one part of the Napoleon rule in play.

A great example of both parts of the Napoleon rule being used in one advertising campaign is the manufactured pandemonium of Black Friday in the United States. Never have I seen so many people behave in such a frantic and emotional way, waiting in line outside the store before it opens. When the doors open, kind, mild-mannered people turn into monsters, all to save $40 on a TV.

What is it about Black Friday that makes people go crazy? Firstly, it appeals to self-interest. Everyone wants a deal. Everyone wants to feel like they are making smart choices with their money, even if they are flat broke. Secondly, it appeals to the fear of missing out: while stocks last, in store only, limited doorbuster deals are just some of the tactics retailers use to make people camp outside the night before for fear of missing out. Lastly, it creates a genuine time constraint of being available for one day only. This time constraint polarizes people into either taking action now or not buying at all. There is no let me think about it, or I will wait until next week. This marketing cocktail of self-interest and the fear of missing out has turned Black Friday into the biggest shopping day of the year.

Now that you know the secret of the Napoleon rule, you will start to see advertising in a whole new way. You will be able to instantly tell when the Napoleon rule is being used and witness its power in full effect.

Key Takeaway #5

Fear and self-interest drive almost all decisions we make.

HOW TO CREATE LOVE AT FIRST SIGHT

The idea of love at first sight is something that we all dream of experiencing. Some may call it lust, but whatever the feeling is, the result is the same: a deep emotional connection that captures that person's full attention.

Whether or not you have experienced love at first sight you have probably experienced a situation where you meet someone or see something that takes your full attention. This feeling makes you feel that this person or this experience was made just for you. Creating a "that's for me" reaction is all about mastering the first impression. It's also about polarizing the person's emotional state. You want them to either love you or hate you. The emotion you want to avoid at all cost is indifference.

Creating a "that's for me" reaction is broken up into two parts. Firstly, you must capture the person's attention and, secondly, you must compel them to stop what they are doing and take action.

So, how do we create a "that's for me" reaction with our marketing campaigns? How do we make people fall in love with what we have to offer the first time they see it? We do this by mastering the first impression. The first impression in your marketing campaigns is the headline.

This is the single most important part of any advertising. The legendary direct response marketer David Ogilvy once said:

"On the average, five times as many people read the headline as read the body copy. When you have written your headline, you have spent eighty cents out of your dollar."

— David Ogilvy

When you are writing sales copy you should spend five times as much time working on the headline as you do on the body copy. Most people will read every word of the headline but only skim the body copy.

Writing a headline that creates a "that's for me" reaction is broken up into two parts. Firstly, you must capture the person's attention and, secondly, you must compel them to stop what they are doing and take action.

How do we take their attention and persuade them to take action, all in one sentence?

Think of a headline as the beginning of a conversation between you and your audience. What can you do to help them? What is the one thing your audience is struggling to do that you have the remedy for?

Remember, people want instant gratification. So, don't make the marketing message complicated. Simple headlines outperform tricky headlines every single time.

Your product or service is the shortcut, not the detour.

A great starting point for writing headlines that convert clicks into customers is to follow a formula. I know what you are thinking—you don't like the idea of using a formula because you want your headlines to be original. Direct response marketing is not about being creative, it's about being effective. Marketers that turn advertising into profit rely on proven principles, not subjective creativity. The formulas I am about to share with you have already been tested; they work, and they will work for you too. One of the great things about direct response marketing is that you can learn from other people's mistakes and from other people's victories. When you use proven formulas, you use other people's marketing tests to your advantage.

Formula Number One

How to + (Benefit)

1. How to save money on your car insurance
2. How to get cheap tickets to Las Vegas shows
3. How to save money on your credit card

Simple and to the point. Think of how your product helps people and create a how-to headline from that. I can't tell you the number of times a headline as simple as this has outperformed some tricky or funny headline people have to think twice about.

Formula Number Two

How to + (Benefit) + (Without Negative)

1. How to save money on your car insurance without changing insurance companies
2. How to get cheap tickets to Las Vegas shows without waiting in line
3. How to save money on your credit card without getting a new one

By telling your audience that what you have to offer can benefit them without the expected downside you are instantly removing the first objection. Give them something of value without taking something away. That is a two-punch marketing combination that is very hard to ignore.

Remember, everyone wants six-pack abs, but nobody wants to do any sit-ups.

Formula Number Three

(Number) Ways to (Benefit)

1. Five ways to save money on health insurance
2. Seven ways to get a higher credit score
3. Three ways to get a hotel upgrade without paying for it

There is a reason you see list headlines in all over the internet. They work extremely well. People love simplicity and that's what a list is offering. No fluff, no filler, just a short list of ways to achieve the desired outcome. Some of the biggest media companies in the world have built their entire business around this simple but powerful headline formula. There are creative ways to amplify list headlines, but first I would stick with this simple formula for quick and easy success.

Formula Number Four

(Number) Mistakes (A Type of Person) Makes When (Activity)

1. Four mistakes dog owners make when looking for a vet
2. Three mistakes personal trainers make when training older clients
3. Eight mistakes poker players make when sitting at the table

This is a more advanced version of the list headline. The two main differences here are that you are going negative by highlighting mistakes, but more importantly, you are calling out a specific group of people. In the example above you are not talking to pet owners, only dog owners. The more specific you make the headline, the more powerful the response rate will be. Use this headline formula only after you have seen success with the basic list headline. Having the simple headline to test against is a great marketing lesson to learn from.

Formula Number Five

The Truth About (A Subject of Uncertainty)

1. The truth about mortgage brokers
2. The truth about low interest credit cards
3. The truth about last-minute cruise ship deals

This headline formula plays on the audience's curiosity and insecurity about a subject that they are dealing with but don't know enough about. This formula works particularly well for matters that relate to money and that involve some level of risk. This headline formula puts the reader's mind at ease, while at the same time positioning you as someone that is an expert.

Key Takeaway #6

Your product or service is the shortcut, not the detour.

THE MOST IMPORTANT QUESTION IN MARKETING

When you first start creating marketing campaigns, so many questions come to the front of your mind.

What should I say first?

When should I talk about price?

What do I need to do to make them feel like they can trust me?

These are important questions. But these questions

can wait until later. Before we do anything, we need to ask ourselves one very important question. In my experience, this is the most important question when marketing a product. In fact, this could even be the most important question that impacts the success of your business.

What is the number one marketing question?

What are we really selling?

Before you can craft a winning marketing message, you must first understand what you are actually selling.

When you strip this product or service down to its core, what is the ideal outcome people are looking for? Let me give you an example.

Take the fitness industry; a major part of their business is selling gym memberships. If you strip a gym membership down to its core, what is it?

A gym membership is access to a room with exercise equipment in it. That would be a simple description of the main feature of having a gym membership. Nobody buys a gym membership so they can use a treadmill. They buy the benefits of what using a treadmill will offer them.

The benefits of a product or service is the ideal results of someone buying it. The features are what the product is or what it does. Always focus on the end benefits to the user, not the features.

This is the secret sauce behind the most important marketing question.

So, back to our example of gym membership. What are they really selling?

- Gym memberships are selling confidence.

- Gym memberships are selling stress relief.
- Gym memberships are selling sexual desirability.
- Gym memberships are selling are a better version of yourself.
- Gym memberships are selling the body you had when you were younger.
- Gym memberships are selling a reduction in back pain.
- Gym memberships are selling you a better night's sleep.

The list goes on and on, but you get the idea.

Notice that not once did I mention that the gym is open 24 hours or that we just purchased some new equipment or that we offer clean towels to all our guests.

Why? Because you don't buy a gym membership because you want to train late at night or because you are looking for clean towels.

I will give you one more example.

Take one of the most boring and dull products you could imagine, like a carpet cleaning service. Now, on first glance, you could say that they make your carpets clean and smell nice, which is true, but from my experience that is not why most people get their carpets steam cleaned.

A major reason people get their carpets steam cleaned is because they are looking to get the bond back from the landlord.

Another reason to get your carpets cleaned is that it improves the air quality in your house, which reduces the chance that you and your family get sick from airborne bacteria and diseases.

Which offer is more powerful?

Make your carpets so clean they smell like new.
Increase the chance of getting your bond back by 78% in less than two hours.

Or, consider this:

Steam cleaning carpets will remove pet odors.
Protect your newborn baby from hidden airborne bacteria and diseases.

Hopefully, by now you agree that selling benefits, not features, will be one of the keys to your success. Remember, before you do anything ask yourself: What are we really selling?

Now, it's your turn. Take your product or service and list the features—meaning what the product does or has to offer. Then take those features and turn them into benefits.

Key Takeaway #6

Sell the emotional reason someone would buy your product, then justify that emotion with logic.

THE 4 STEPS TO CREATING A COMPELLING OFFER

Very few people know how to sell. Even fewer people can explain how they do it. How do you craft a compelling offer each and every time? Could you take a random product or service and craft a compelling offer in less than one hour? Odds are the answer is no. The only reason why you don't know how to sell is that you don't know the formula. Understanding the sales process starts with breaking it down into just four easy steps.

1) Pre-qualify the audience

If I told you I was going to sell hot dogs outside a vegan convention, you would tell me that you think I'm crazy. Which makes sense, right — I'm trying to sell a product to people that have no interest in buying it.

One of the biggest red flags I hear is when people say that their product is for everyone. If your product is for everyone, then you don't know the customer well enough yet.

Don't fall for the marketing lie that anyone can be sold any product with the right pitch. That is completely false. Even if you are giving your product away for free, they still have to want to take it. That's why one of the biggest mistakes I see people make is selling to people that have no interest in the product.

I know what you are thinking, but Josh the only

reason they don't want to buy my product is because they have not tried it yet. Wrong. Your offer should speak to a specific person, not everyone.

Do yourself a massive favor and target your advertising to that one person your product can help, not a group of people. When you are writing the ad copy it helps to imagine you are speaking to the person one-on-one. That way, the tone of the copy that you write sounds like a conversation you would have in a coffee shop.

So, how do we pre-qualify the audience?

Pre-qualifying the audience is done in two ways. Firstly, by targeting ads to the specific group of people that you are trying to help. The way in which you target ads changes all the time. We will discuss targeting later in this book. What we want to focus on right now is the second way you can pre-qualify your audience.

The fastest, most effective way to pre-qualify an audience is to make an opening statement that instantly polarizes them. You want to let your audience know as soon as possible what you have and how you can help them. This sounds like common sense, but let me tell you, common sense is not common. So many people make broad opening statements with their advertising in the hope of casting the widest net.

Casting a wide net means you need to be very general and vague in how you describe your product. People do not make buying decisions with general information.

The goal is not to cast the widest net but to bait the perfect hook.

Speak to that single person about a very specific problem. Crafting a sales message this way creates a love it or leave it reaction with your audience.

This is what we want.

We want our audience to feel like the product is made just for them. Even though human beings are pack animals, most people like to think of themselves as one of a kind with unique needs and perspectives.

Here are some examples of bad opening statements and how we can easily fix them.

Example 1:
Bad Headline:
Lose weight this summer, win $5000.

Better Headline:
New mothers weight loss challenge. Win $5000.

This new headline instantly pre-qualifies the prospect to new mothers looking to lose the weight after having a baby. You could also intensify the headline by creating some urgency by adding a deadline like "entries close today at 6 p.m."

Example 2:

Bad headline:
Save money on your next weekend getaway.

Better Headline:
Instantly save 25% off your next trip to Las Vegas.

Again, we make the offer much more powerful by targeting a single group of people — people looking to book a trip to Vegas. Even more, instantly increase the power of the offer by defining the exact saving the person is going to get by taking you up on the offer.

By now, I hope you understand the importance of pre-qualifying the audience when crafting a sales message. Stop selling to people that have no interest in buying your product. All you are doing is wasting your valuable advertising dollars. Start every conversation with your audience as if you are speaking to them one-on-one. You will get a much stronger response by doing this and, for the rest of the sales message, you will know exactly who you are speaking to.

Key Takeaway #8

The goal is not to cast the widest net but to bait the perfect hook.

2) Define the problem

After you have pre-qualified the audience, it's time to define the problem. The easiest way to define the problem is by focusing on what this problem is costing this person. Is it putting their life at risk? Is it costing them money that they didn't even know about? Clearly defining the problem is about finding the pain point and hammering on it.

Remember, if you find your customer's pain, you will find their wallet.

The best way to define the problem is to tell a realistic and relatable story that speaks to that person's own experience. The key thing here is not to start just making things up or to take the story to a place that very few members of your audience have experienced. We keep the story realistic because, first and foremost, it means that you build long-term trust with your audience. Telling lies is not the way to win people over or build a strong brand long-term.

The second and strategic reason for making the story realistic is because it makes the story easier to relate to. People like people who are like themselves.

Describe your target audience's situation in a way that feels like you are having a conversation with them. The trick here is to go into as much detail as possible. If you are selling a product about weight loss, talk about the specific situation that caused you either physical or emotional harm. Speak from the heart — the audience will listen.

One thing I have discovered in my own experience writing and testing sales copy for different products is that the tone of sales copy has a massive impact on conversion rates. The key takeaway here is that your copy should be different for the type of problem you are trying to solve.

If your product is offering help for a personal problem that has been caused mostly by their own actions, or inaction, for that matter, it's important to never, under any circumstances, blame or point the finger at them as the cause of the problem. Even if it is their fault. It does you no favors, making them feel guilty. Anyway, if they are the problem, why do they need you?

When telling a story about how to solve a personal problem, use softer language. Make them feel like they are not alone. Make them feel that they should not lose hope. Most importantly, make them feel that they still have a chance to turn things around.

On the other hand, if you are selling a product that solves a problem that is not caused by your target customer's actions but by someone else's, you can let all hell break loose. They are angry and sick to death of the situation, and so should you be.Use short sentences. Use slang words that you would never use in a formal conversation.

Most importantly, make sure you create a common enemy in the mind of the prospect. Here are some examples.

- How greedy credit cards companies are ripping you off, and what you can do to stop it.

- How one woman outsmarted one of the world's largest insurance companies.
- Did you pay this hidden fee in your tax return last year?
- What my $580-per-hour accountant taught me about saving money on tax returns.

Each of these headlines tells a story. Each one of these headlines makes the reader feel like they are not the only one that has this problem.

If you know your customer and how your product can help that person, this story should write itself.

There is one last thing to remember about telling a story that defines the problem. This is often where you can lose people. You must make the story entertaining and compelling. Each sentence should be selling the reader on reading more.

The opening paragraph is make or break. Think of

the first few lines as a sales pitch for the rest of the story. Lead with something worth listening to. This is easier said than done. Get in the habit of learning new ways to open a story in only a few words.

Becoming a better storyteller will open more doors for you than you ever thought possible. You know that person who is the life of the party and everyone hangs on their every word? They are great storytellers, and becoming a better storyteller will make your customers like you faster than you ever thought possible.

If you are having trouble putting the story together (which is completely normal, by the way) don't stress out about that at all. Ask yourself the following questions to help get the creative juices flowing:

- Who is this person?
- What do they do for a living?

- What do they spend their spare time doing?

- How long, on average, have they had this problem?

- What is this problem costing them in the short term?

- What is this problem costing them in the long term?

- What is the worst thing that can happen if this problem is not fixed?

3) Offer a solution

So you have pre-qualified the audience and defined the problem, now what? Time to offer a solution. This is the time when your product takes full focus. By now, if your reader is still with you, they are interested in what you have to offer. All you need to do is craft the offer in a way that makes them feel they are getting more than they are giving. It may sound simple, but it isn't.

How do we demonstrate value to a pre-qualified audience with a very specific problem? We follow the same formula that got us here. Firstly, we speak directly to the person as if they are sitting next to us. We are having a personal conversation with a friend, not the audience of a stadium.

Secondly, we explain how what we have to offer fixes the problem they are trying to solve. Like we discussed in an earlier chapter, we always focus on what is in it for them. We do not talk about how good we are. We only talk about how we can help them. The audience does not care about you, they only care about what you can do for them.

Speaking directly to your target customer's own interests is perhaps the most powerful thing you can do.

By now you are probably thinking, how do I talk about how I can help my audience without mentioning how good I am?

Describing in detail how you can help that person with their problem is telling them what to hear. When done right, this will position you as someone that is an authority on the subject, which in turn makes you someone that they want to do business with.

An easy way to describe your product in a way that both explains what the product is but also sells the benefits is this simple formula.

(What it Does) + (So You Can) + (Benefit)

Here are some examples:

- We guarantee to arrive within 30 mins, so you can get on with the rest of your day.

- Now with twice the protein so you can feel fuller for longer.
- 16% increase in battery life so you can leave your charger at home.
- Save 25% on hotel rooms so you can spend more going shopping.

There are two important things to remember when talking about your product or service.

The first thing you need to remember is that you should always be talking about the benefits of the product, not the features. Features are what the product does. The benefits are why you care. Even if we are selling a highly technical product with a long list of features, it is our job as marketers to convert technical features into end user benefits. People buy based on emotion and justify that purchase with logic.

Leading the conversation with the benefits of the product starts an emotional conversation in the mind of the prospect. More than anything else, people buy emotional states. Buying a new outfit makes most people feel more confident. If people only bought based on logic, no one in their right mind would ever pay $5000 for a suit or $35,000 for a watch.

Describe the emotional state that your product offers your customer. This idea alone can dramatically increase conversion rates.

Remember, sell the benefit, sell the emotional state, and never sell the feature.

The second important thing to remember is that you have to prove the negative voices in the customer's mind wrong. No one will believe you unless you can show them proof. People have become very skeptical when they hear marketing offers. Don't take it personally. I'm sure your product is great and does exactly what you say it does. When it comes to marketing, a few bad apples affect an entire industry.

So, how do we get around the problem of new customers not believing us?

When we talk about our product, the proof that it works should be one of the main messages you give your customers. Demonstrating proof that your product does what you say it does is often the determining factor in the success of advertising.

The burden of proof is squarely on your shoulders. One important question to think about is, what must we demonstrate to be true in order for people to be willing to do business with us?

In summary, offering the solution to your target customer's problem should be much easier now that you understand what to focus on. Speak to them like it's a personal conversation. Sell the benefits of the product, not the features. Last, but not least, overcome the first mental objection by demonstrating proof that your product can do what you say it can and help your customer, just like it has helped other people in the past.

4) Tell them what to do next

The last step in creating a compelling offer is to tell them what to do next. If you have completed the first three steps properly this should feel very natural for both you and your customers.

You already know who you are talking to because you have already pre-qualified them. They already know who you are because they have listened to your story and decided to continue the conversation. They have heard about the solution you have to offer, and they want to hear more. Depending on how well you did in defining the problem and offering a solution, you may even have built a base level of trust with your target audience.

A compelling offer is the exchange of value.

If you have demonstrated enough value, what you tell them to do next is less important than you realize. Don't kid yourself and think that you can trick people into buying something.

Telling them what to do next is often called "a call to action". All that means is that you are now directly telling them to do something in order to get something. Telling them what to do next can be as simple as an "order now" button on your website or as complicated as filling out an application process.

A simple and easy way to tell them what to do next is to offer them the same help you have given people in the past. This time, reduce the risk to them upfront.

Just to be clear, I am not saying that you should sell yourself short. What I am saying is that you should reduce the risk or pain to the customer if things don't work out.

Don't think that this means you have to discount your product in any way. You can charge any price you want. Truth be told, if you have followed the first three steps of the process you should be in a position to charge more for your product because your marketing message is now stronger and you have demonstrated more value.

All we need to do is offer a safety net. Can you return the product if they do not like it? Do you offer a 30-day money back guarantee? How long is the warranty for? Could you make it longer without any real impact on your business? These are the questions you should be asking yourself.

If you are selling a professional service that tends to have a higher ticket price, you will have much greater success if you remove any roadblocks people might have to why they would reach out to you for the first time. Would you be willing to offer a 30-minute discovery session at no cost to the client? If this is going to be a long-term business relationship you will benefit from getting to know the client before you start billing hours to them.

I know what you are thinking — what about all the people that are going to waste your time if you start giving away 30-minute discovery sessions? The best way to get around this is to have a screening process that weeds out all the time wasters. As a general rule, most professional service companies ask the same questions in the opening five minutes of a sales call. If you transfer those questions to an online form, you can have all of the major high-level questions answered before you even take the call.

Doing it this way may generate few calls, but the calls you do have will be of a much higher quality, which is what you are most likely looking for anyway.

At the end of the discovery call, be sure to mention the price of your services. Don't waste your time creating complicated proposals only to find that the client's budget is not worth your time.

One mistake I see people make all the time is asking the client what budget they have for the project. Just to be clear, you set the prices for your services, not your clients. When you open the conversation about pricing by asking what the client is looking to pay, you put yourself at a massive disadvantage. Respected companies have written price lists. So should you. When pricing is left up to the client to decide, you will always be shortchanged.

One last thing about pricing for professional services. Whenever you present pricing to a client, and they start giving you low-ball offers, take that as a massive red flag. Negotiations within reason is fine. Extending the term of the contract for a small discount is fine. However, when the client starts telling you they have champagne tastes on a beer budget, respectfully decline the project. These people are problem clients, and you don't want them in your business.

I hope that by now you understand that telling the audience what do next is only natural. You are here to help people, you are here to lead them to a better outcome. All you need to do now is reduce the risks to the customer if they don't like you. Hopefully, this is only the first sale of many with the client.

In summary, here are the four steps to creating a compelling offer:

1. Pre-qualify the audience

Who are you targeting? Create an opening statement that instantly polarizes your audience. You want to target your message to a very specific person, not a broad group of people.

2. Define the problem

Clearly define the problem that you are solving. What is the cost to your target customer? Share a relatable story with the reader that makes them feel that they are not alone, and that other people just like them have turned things around.

3. Offer a solution

How can you solve this problem better than they can? This is where you introduce your product or service. Sell the benefits of the product, not the features. Remember that the burden of proof is on you to make the audience believe that it does what you say it does. One important question to think about when talking about your product is what do I have to prove to be true for my customers to want to be business with me?

4. Tell them what to do next

Now is the time to lead the audience to a better outcome, the call to action. This can be asking them to place an order, or it could be simply asking them to call you. You will greatly increase the number of people that contact you if you can reduce or eliminate the risk to them if they are wrong.

There you have it. The four steps to creating a compelling offer.

The more you do this, the better you will get. Here's a practice exercise – take a product that you are not familiar with and craft a marketing message for it.

THE FASTEST WAY TO TURN CUSTOMERS AWAY

People don't have time to read between the lines or to dig deeper into a marketing message. It must grab them within the first few seconds, or your customers are gone forever. The fastest way to turn people away is to make your offer vague and open to interpretation.

- Does your opening statement create more follow-up questions?

- Are you making a vague general statement because you hope to attract the largest audience?
- Are you making your product messaging a riddle that the audience has to solve?

Let me tell you one thing for certain. People do not make buying decisions based on general information. People want details. They want to know exactly how you can help them.

Leading with general statements like "we are cheaper" or "we are faster" is only adding to the marketing noise they hear every day. Also, stop trying to cast the widest net. Effective marketing is not about casting the widest net. It's about baiting the perfect hook. Remember, we are not looking to help everyone, but rather we are looking to help a very specific person with a very specific problem.

Another important reason to make your offers as specific as possible is that people don't want to invest time decoding what your product does and how it can help them. Remember, everyone is short on time, so you must demonstrate specific and measurable value upfront if you want people to do business with you.

Consider these two offers:

1. Mother's Day Sale this weekend.
2. Mother's Day Sale this weekend. 40% off everything storewide.

Which offer is more powerful?

The more specific your offer is, the greater the conversion rate will be. This is even more important if you are selling a complicated product or if your product has a high price tag. The more information you give your audience, the more money they will give you. Sounds like a pretty good deal, right?

The main problem with making vague general statements with your marketing is that it creates doubt in the customer's mind. They already have doubts, so don't add new ones.

Another great way to sharpen your marketing message is to make your opening statement an answer to a frequently asked question by one of your clients or your target audience. This style of marketing is best used in markets where you have clearly defined problems. What I mean by that is, you are helping them with a very urgent problem that is top of mind.

Review your marketing messaging. Are you turning people away by making vague promises? If you could make your opening statement simple and direct, what would you say?

Key takeaway #9

The more direct and specific your marketing message is, the greater the conversion rate will be. The more information you give them, the more money they will give you.

WHAT LEONARDO DA VINCI TAUGHT ME ABOUT MARKETING

It has been said that no single man in human history knew more than Leonardo da Vinci.

Most historians agree that Leonardo da Vinci was one of the most important minds that ever lived. Leonardo defined the term "Renaissance Man". Most people only know him as a master painter, but he was a master of so much more.

Leonardo da Vinci is what is now known as a polymath. A polymath is someone that has a vast depth of knowledge in a number of different subject areas. Such a person can draw on seemingly unrelated areas of knowledge to solve very complex problems in a way that even experts in that field did not think possible. Galileo was another famous polymath.

Leonardo da Vinci described himself as someone that had an unquenchable curiosity about the world around him. He was fascinated by human anatomy and how that compares to the anatomy of birds, which led to his invention of the helicopter and the parachute 500 years ahead of his time. This is an example of how he used his knowledge of two different areas of expertise to create something that no one at the time had ever thought of.

He studied painting, science, mathematics, and engineering. He was someone that was constantly connecting the dots. His study of the relationship between mathematics and music is another great example of how his mind saw connections.

Through his extensive studies, he witnessed recurring themes and principles that were present in almost all of the subjects that drew his interest. One of these principles was the idea of simplicity.

Leonardo Da Vinci famously said:

"Simplicity is the ultimate sophistication."

What he observed was that the most visually appealing design is often very simple. His appreciation for simplicity led him to design some of the most beautiful artworks in human history.

How does Leonardo da Vinci's appreciation for simplicity help us become better marketers?

Our goal as marketers should be to use the laws of human nature to our advantage. If the human mind is on a constant search for simplicity, our aim should be to make our offer to our customers as simple as possible.

It's easy to add something extra. The hard part is stripping something down to its core. The challenge is not to add more but to remove what is not completely necessary.

I am a firm believer that there are marketing lessons are everywhere. This is a perfect example of that. Learn from the lessons of history.

Making your marketing message as simple as possible goes a very long way to increasing conversion rates. The simplest solution to the problem wins.

Customers are looking for answers, not new questions.

By making things simple you tell your customers that you have a deep understanding of the problem, and you don't need to bore them with all the extra details.

Making things super complicated means that you haven't done the work to describe your product to the people who need it the most — your customers.

I think my favorite childhood author says it best:

"Sometimes the questions are complicated, but the answers are simple."

— Dr. Seuss

Dr. Seuss understood the power of simple messages, and so do your customers. Simple words cut through the noise. Simple words are easy to remember. Simple images are easy to understand.

It is our job as marketers to turn our customers' problems into simple user benefits.

More times than I can remember, removing something unnecessary has increased conversion rates.

One mistake I see people make is that they use big fancy words in an attempt to make themselves look smart. Stop trying to impress people, and start trying to help people.

Using fancy words or even industry jargon makes you and your product unrelatable to your audience. People buy from people that they can relate to. Do whatever you can to make your customers feel like they are just like you.

Cool, you went to a fancy school and read books that are as thick as a phone book. That is great, but how does that help your customers? Describing your product in a way that makes you sound smart boosts your ego, not your bank account.

Describe your benefits in a way that would remove all follow-up questions. This will bring you one step closer to the sale.

Do yourself a favor and review the advertising material you have created for your product. At any time during the marketing message have you made things complicated?

Did you use fifteen words when you could have used five?

Did anything you say open up new questions in the customer's mind?

Did you use jargon when you could have used a simple word that anyone could understand?

If the answer is yes to the last three questions, go back and write a simpler version that you would not need to explain to someone. Creating a simple version of your marketing message will teach you a great deal about your product and help you craft a better opening message when you describe your product to someone in person.

A great place to start is to explain your product as if you are talking to someone that has zero knowledge of your industry or your product.

Remember what Leonardo da Vinci said: simplicity is the ultimate sophistication.

Key Takeaway #10

If your marketing does not make sense, it will not make dollars.

HOW DO YOU SELL AN IDENTICAL PRODUCT FOR MORE THAN YOUR COMPETITORS?

People often ask me, how do you sell an identical product for more than the competition?

This is easier than you may think. Firstly, the world is full of identical products sold for vastly different prices. The fashion industry is probably the best example of this. Most of the well-known clothing brands in the United States are owned by only a handful of companies. These companies make all of their products in offshore locations. What most people don't realize is that the cheap entry-level products and the luxury products are both made in the same factory, by the same people, often with the exact same materials. How is this done?

By understanding this simple law:

The cost that it takes to create something and the price you sell it at should have nothing to do with each other.

Linking the costs to manufacture a product with the price you sell it for means that you are signing yourself up for a race that nobody wins. This is called the "race to the bottom." Razor-thin margins, zero brand loyalty, and no real long-term business advantage. Josh, that's all well and good in theory, but everyone in my industry charges the same prices. If I increased my prices, I would only scare customers away.

For example, let's take one of the most boring everyday products you could imagine – duct tape. Everyone knows duct tape. Most people have either purchased or used duct tape at some point in their life and have not given it a second thought.

How do we sell a simple product like duct tape for more than you ever thought possible?

This is a three-step process.

1. Define the ultimate end-benefit to the user

In as much detail as possible, what is the best use case you can think of that would deliver the highest benefit in the shortest time? For duct tape, a common use is to repair items cheaply and quickly. Another great benefit of duct tape is that it instantly creates a strong bond with whatever surface it touches. So strong, in fact, that it creates a watertight seal. Without much effort at all, we have just come up with two powerful benefits: it can repair items quickly and with a water-tight seal. Sounds like we are onto something.

2. Create a narrow audience

Can you think a group of people that need a cheap and easy way to repair items that also provides a watertight seal? Boat owners. Boats are expensive and require extensive maintenance to keep them in working order. Boat owners even joke that the two best days of having a boat are the day you buy it and the day you sell it. Most boat owners know that having a boat is basically like having a hole in your pocket. Targeting our new ad campaign to boat owners who are always looking for new ways to save money repairing their boats puts us at a huge advantage.

3. Tell a story that speaks to them

All we need to do now is create an ad that tells a story specifically targeting boat owners. This ad will highlight the pain of the ongoing maintenance costs of having a boat. We could even give an example of how the cost of boat repairs can often be more than the cost of the boat itself. So all we do now is tell them what they want to hear. This can be the following "how one boat owner saved $786 on boat repairs," "how a simple $6 item can save you from the next trip to the boat mechanic," or "how frugal boat owners save money on boat repairs." The ad writes itself.

Now, I'm not saying that all boat repairs can be fixed with duct tape, but small tears and leaks can be. That is the story I would tell in the ad. I would say something like: "Duct tape can't fix everything, but when you are out on the water and need a quick fix to get you back into shore, duct tape has your back".

See what we did there? With the right target audience, paired with a compelling story that highlights the cost savings to boat owners, you could easily sell duct tape for at least twice what people at the hardware store sell it for.

But, what if you are selling a service. You can follow the same three-step process, but this time define the benefits of your service.

The only thing stopping you from charging more for a similar product or service than your competitors is the quality of your marketing. If you double the quality of your marketing message, you can easily increase the cost of your product.

Take the time now to ask yourself the following questions:

- What is the best-case scenario for my product or service?
- What type of person could benefit from my product or service the most?

- What other more expensive products could I link with my product to instantly raise the value of it in my prospect's mind?

- What story could I tell that would compel the right target audience to pay more for my product?

HOW TO INCREASE YOUR PRICES WITHOUT CUSTOMERS PUSHING BACK

It's crazy how your personal life can teach you lessons about your professional life even if you are not ready to hear it. I have learnt to accept this now. I look for marketing lessons everywhere I go.

The first time this happened, it took me by surprise, but it had a deep and profound impact on the way I see the world and how I market products and services.

I had a health scare a few years ago which led me to a visit with my local family doctor. The night before I had noticed something that was not right, and I knew I needed someone to look at it right away. I didn't sleep well that night. My mind was racing with all the possibilities of what could be wrong.

The next day I woke up early, canceled my morning plans, and made my way to my local doctor. I was lucky to be one of the first patients in the door that day. After waiting around 20 minutes, I was in front of the doctor describing what I thought was wrong with my body. After the doctor's careful inspection, he recommended scans to be completed and that I see a specialist.

By this time, my mind was sure that my worst fears had come true. I asked the doctor what the possibilities were, and he told me that this could be not a problem at all or something very serious. I was very emotional, gripped with fear about what could be happening to me. The one thing he could tell me was that I was not too young for this to happen, and that it was very much possible that it could be life-threatening.

I followed the doctor's orders and got the scans done that day. I then needed to book an appointment with a specialist that deals with conditions like this. However, the earliest appointment he had was a week and a half away. A week and a half felt like much too long for me to wait to get the answers I needed to help me sleep at night.

I didn't sleep very well at all. I didn't really want to do much of anything. Finally, the time came for the appointment, and I arrived early to come and see the specialist. The first thing I noticed was that his waiting room was full of people waiting to see him. I sat down and I waited.

When the time finally came for me to see the specialist, my name was called, and I went and sat down in his office. I passed him the copies of my scans, and he quickly noticed something he had seen before. He smiled, which I thought was a good sign.

He told me there was nothing to worry about and that what I had was not serious. I was overcome by happiness. I then asked a few follow-up questions, which he answered in great detail. By this time, he had completely put my mind at ease.

I shook the specialist's hand, and I was directed to his receptionist to take care of the bill. The bill was not cheap, but I was more than happy to pay it. While I was filling out the form to pay the bill, I checked my watch for the date. I then realized that I had only been in the specialist's office for a little over fifteen minutes. That made me smile, and that's when it hit me.

My family doctor was equally as smart and knowledgeable. He knew vast amounts of information about all different types of illnesses and conditions.You could see him any time. He was your friend, and you respected him. But, when the time came for a serious medical condition, he would refer you on to a specialist.

The specialist, on the other hand, was in a very unique position. He was also a doctor but focused on a very specific medical condition, which meant that his time was extremely valuable. You couldn't just walk in a see him, you first needed to have a referral, and then schedule an appointment according to his timetable, not yours.

This put the specialist in a position to work the hours he wanted on his terms. He didn't have to offer house calls or even late office hours.

But, most importantly, the specialist could charge whatever he liked, and people would be happy to pay it. I know I was. In fact, if I had had the option to see the specialist sooner for an extra fee I would have paid it in a heartbeat.

You should always position yourself as a specialist in whatever it is that you do. Don't make the mistake of being yet another person in your industry that is a jack of all trades but a master of none.

Becoming a specialist opens doors that someone with general skills could never open. Becoming a specialist tells the world in no uncertain terms that you know more than they do about this topic, and when you say something they'd better listen and take notes.

Don't make the mistake of becoming a generalist in your marketplace. The economy of tomorrow does not need more people that have simply scratched the surface. It needs people that have taken the time to dig deep and have developed a complete understanding of the topic on hand.

Simply by taking the time to position yourself as a specialist will achieve two extremely powerful things almost instantly:

1) It will enable you to increase your prices without any pushback from your customers. In fact, they

will be happy to pay more knowing that they have an expert fixing their problems.

2) You will attract a higher quality of customer that respects your time and is willing to follow the advice that you give them.

The last benefit I would like to mention about becoming a specialist is that when the market takes a turn for the worse, and companies are looking to scale back on spending, you will be the last person they will look to get rid of because of your unique set of skills and expertises would   be very hard to replace.

Demonstrating to the world that you are a specialist will increase your conversion rates because people want the peace of mind of knowing that they have an expert working with them to fix their problems.

THE TRUTH ABOUT TRUST

In this last chapter of the marketing section of this book, I need to tell you something that I think is extremely important and something that is not discussed enough within marketing circles and marketing training in general. I want to talk about the important relationship you have with your customers and how this relationship boils down to one thing:

Trust.

When you lose the trust of your customers, you lose the ability to do business with them ever again. The relationship you have with your customers is very much like the relationships you have in your personal life. Treat people with respect and see things from their point of view, and you will have friends that want to spend time with you.

The key takeaway from this chapter is the understanding that the currency in which we build trust is honesty. Tell the truth to your customers, even if it means potentially losing the sale upfront, but in the long term building a relationship that benefits you for years to come.

Some of the principles in this book when in the wrong hands or used with the wrong intentions can make people do things that are not in their best interest. Please do not do that.

Just so I make myself clear, do not bend the truth or over exaggerate the benefits of your product. Your customers will see through that and not want to do business with you. Worst of all, if they do business with and you, and they feel like you have cheated them, you have hell to pay.

Please remember that people are much more likely to leave negative reviews than positive ones, so don't give them a reason to leave you a negative review. It will hurt you today and in the long term.

Give people a reason to leave you a positive review. Always tell the truth with your marketing statements. No exceptions.

One of the biggest mistakes I see people make with marketing and business in general is that they don't think long term. What is good for you in the short term could be very bad for you in the long term. Don't trade a short-term win for a long-term loss.

Lastly, please understand that your reputation is what people say about you when you are not around. Make your reputation something to be proud of, and you will have a long and successful business life. I think Warren Buffet says it best:

"It takes 20 years to build a reputation and five minutes to ruin it. If you think about that, you'll do things differently."

— Warren Buffett

Always tell the truth with your marketing statements. Your customers will thank you for it.

PART TWO: DESIGN

THE GOAL OF LEARNING DESIGN

The goal of this section of the book is not to make you a designer or to teach you how to use graphic design software. The goal is to teach you the fundamental design principles that will increase conversion rates.

With an understanding of these principles, you will be in a much better position to work with a talented designer that can create designs that are both visually appealing but also function in a way that increases the chances that your audience will respond to your marketing statements.

The design of a website has a massive impact on how the website performs, but not in the way that you think.

This is not about creating sites that look like you could win a design award. This is about focusing on user experience and layout design. I personally have no interest in winning design awards. The only award that matters is the money that your customers award you when you have delivered a great product or service. Everything else is simply for the ego.

After you read this section, you will be to work with a designer to create a website that looks great but, more importantly, converts the visitors into customers.

THE MOST IMPORTANT SECTION OF THE WEBSITE

The first and most important design concept I want to share with you that has a direct impact on conversion rates is a design term called "above the fold".

The term above the fold refers to any and all content that the user sees before that user has the option to scroll. This is the content that the user sees before they see anything else. The content above the fold is the area in which you make your first impression.

This term was originally used in newspaper ads but

has stuck around in the digital age. Above the fold for a newspaper is the top section of the newspaper that will display on newsstands. Newspaper owners, even to this day, place the utmost focus on the content above the fold. They know it's the most important real estate of the newspaper, and that's why they charge advertisers extra for placing ads in this exclusive area.

The area above the fold is the section of your website that gets the most visibility. This is where your headline is placed. This is where you place your sales video. Any information that is in this area is going to get the most eyeballs on it.

One of the biggest design mistakes I see people make is that they put the important content that would hook the audience below the fold. The content above the fold should be able to communicate to the audience what you do and sell them on taking action to either contact you for more information or to place an order.

How do you measure the area above the fold? Below are some standard measurements of what is generally considered above the fold for both websites and mobile.

Desktop is 1024x786 pixels
Mobile is 375x367 pixels
Tablet is 768x1024 pixels

Take these measurements as a general guide; screen sizes change and so do the above the fold measurements. Additionally, to test if your content is above the fold, Google Chrome has a feature built into the browser that can display a preview of how your website will look on different screen sizes.

How does this work? You don't have to download anything extra. This feature is built-in as a default. Simply right-click anywhere on the webpage and select "inspect" from the list of options. This will bring up a pop-up window at the bottom of the page. Then click on the toggle device toolbar icon located on the top left-hand corner of this pop-up window.

After you click on the toggle device toolbar icon, you will see the screen size in your browser change. There is a drop-down menu at the top of the page above the preview window that will let you choose different screen size options. The screen size options will list different types of mobile phone screen sizes and also offer desktop and tablet previews. If for some reason you would like to preview a custom screen size, you can do that simply by manually entering in the numbers that you want the screen size to change to.

Remember, the most important section of the website is the area above the fold. Keeping this design concept in mind will increase your conversion rates by putting all of the important information in front of as many people as possible.

HOW COLORS IMPACT CONVERSION RATES

The colors you use in your advertising tell the audience a story about your product before they have even read one word of your sales copy. Humans are emotional creatures. Even if we don't like to admit it, more often than not we make decisions based on emotion rather than logic.

It has been said that people buy for emotional reasons and then later justify this emotional purchase with logic. In my experience, this is true. Emotional buying decisions play a much larger role when the product has a high price tag. This sounds crazy, right? This should be the opposite.

Very few people buy luxury products for logical reasons.

Luxury is about how it makes you feel, not how it makes you think. The only thinking that matters when buying luxury products is the way other people will think of you when they see you with that luxury item. Understanding the real reason why people buy a product will greatly increase the chances of your success in selling them that product.

Don't get me wrong, I love luxury products and buy them all the time, but as a marketer, I can't help but ask myself why I pay extra for a product that I can't justify with logic.

So, how do we tell a story about our product before we even open our mouths? One way is the colors we use in the branding and layout of our website. The colors you decide upon have a massive impact on the way your potential customers feel about your product.

Every color tells a story, so decide carefully what type of story you want to tell. Deciding on the colors you want to use for your product is heavy influenced by the type of product you are selling and the demographics of the person you are aiming to sell your product to.

Below is a summary of some feelings that colors create when used in advertising.

Red

Red is the color of emotional extremes. Red is the color of primal desires and deeply emotional experiences. Red is also the color of fire and blood. Intense things happen with the color red. Lust and sexual desire are often linked with the color red.

Not surprisingly, red is one of the top favorite colors of all people. On another note, red is also on over 70% of all international flags from all around the world.

Red in Asian culture is the color of good luck. Brides in both China and India get married in red dresses. On the other hand, red is also the color used in the stock market to signify loss or risk. In summary, red is a color that gets people's attention.

Some examples of companies that you use red in their logo and branding are Coca-Cola, McDonald's, and Toyota. Large media companies such as CNN and Netflix also use red in their logo.

Yellow
Yellow is the color of happiness, creativity, and optimism. Yellow is the color of spring and positive change.

In the natural world, yellow is the color of vibrant life, lemons, and flowers. In the digital world, yellow is the color of happy faces and laughing. On the other hand, yellow also alerts us to trouble or danger. Road signs are almost always yellow.

Yellow also has a dark side. Yellow is the color of

cowardice and betrayal. Yellow is also the color of physical illness. Using the color yellow needs special consideration. While small sections of yellow can easily take over the page, you can also use this to your advantage to highlight a section of the page that you want your audience to focus on.

Some examples of companies that use yellow in their logo and branding are Ikea, Best Buy, and Nikon. National Geographic also use yellow in their branding.

Blue

Blue is the most popular color in the world. Blue is the color of the sky and the ocean. Blue is the color of heaven and authority.

Above all, blue is the color of trust and integrity. Blue is the number one color used by banks and financial institutions in their branding and logos. Blue is also the color of intelligence. The color blue has been often linked with wealth and power. People from wealthy families are considered to be people of blue blood.

If your product or service is something that requires the customer to give you a great deal of trust, incorporating blue into your logo and branding would be a good place to start.

Some examples of companies that use blue in their logo and branding are Facebook, Visa, and IBM. PayPal and American Express also use blue in their logo.

Green

Green is the color of new beginnings and growth. Green is the color of nature and the outdoors. Green is the color associated with progress and moving forward. Traffic lights and good notification symbols are always green.

Interestingly enough, green is also the color of inexperience and lack of technical skill. To describe someone in a business environment as green it means that they are new and don't have any hands-on experience in what they are doing.

Green is also the color of jealousy and envy. Depending on which country in the world you call home, green can be either lucky like in Ireland or unlucky, like in Australia.

Some examples of companies that use green in their logo and branding are Whole Foods Market, Holiday Inn, and Starbucks. Land Rover and Heineken also use green in their logo.

Orange

Orange is the color of excitement. Orange is the color of fire and flame. Orange is the color of extremes. It is also the color of caution and of slowing down to think and consider things.

Since orange is such a bright color, it has also been known for indicating poor taste or a lack of sophistication. Studies have shown a link between the color orange and products that are cheap or of low quality.

Make sure to carefully consider using orange as the main color of your branding. Orange is often best suited as a color that highlights areas of focus, not the main color of a website.

Some examples of companies that use orange in their logo and branding are Harley-Davidson, TNT, and Fanta. Nickelodeon also use orange in their logo.

Purple

Purple is traditionally the color of nobility and luxury. In modern times this is changing, but people from older generations or religious groups link the color purple with religious significance.

Purple is a color that people either love or hate. Very few things found in the natural world are the color purple, so that creates the idea of rarity. Modern video games use the color purple to identify a rare and powerful item in the game.

Purple means different things to different people,

mostly because of their age. It's best to consider the age of your target customer when using purple in your website or advertising material.

Some examples of companies that use purple in their logo and branding are Hallmark, Cadbury, and Yahoo. Fedex also use purple in their branding.

Now that you know how colors make you feel, you will be much better equipped to communicate to your target audience about what your product represents before you even say one word about your product.

THE PROBLEM WITH CHOICE

When I was as a kid, my favorite holiday was Christmas Day, of course.What kid does not love Christmas Day?

My second favorite day was every single Tuesday. Why Tuesday? Every Tuesday our local video shop would offer a special deal where you could rent five video games for seven days for only $10. Every week my mum would take us to the video store, and we would bring home five new video games to play. Our local video store had a massive selection of video games and it would often take a very long time to go through each area, looking at the new and old titles.

I spent a great deal of time at that video store, checking out all the new games and thinking about what I would want to play next. The larger the collection at the store grew, the longer it would take for my brothers and I to decide which game we wanted to play.

Fast forward to today. We have streaming services that offer thousands of movies that have cost hundreds of millions of dollars to make, and all we have to pay is around $10 a month. Not bad, right? And all without having to leave the house.

Sounds amazing, right? It is amazing, but do you know what happens? We spend more time looking for something to watch than actually watching something. Ten thousand movies to choose from, but there is nothing on TV worth watching. Sometimes we search for a show for so long we decide we don't want to watch anything at all.

This is the problem with choice. The more choice

we have, the less likely we are to make a decision. This is called the choice overload problem.

Psychologists Sheena Iyengar and Mark Lepper from Columbia and Stanford University, conducted a study in 2000 challenging the idea that more choice had a positive impact on a person's ability to make a decision. In the experiment, they set up a tasting booth near the entrance of a local market selling either 6 or 24 flavors of jam. They looked at two things: in which case were people more likely to sample the jam and in which case were people more likely to buy the jam. First, more people stopped (60%) when there were 24 flavors compared to 6 (40%). However, of the people that stopped when there were 24 flavors, only 3% actually bought the jam. In contrast, of the people that stopped when there were only 6 flavors, about 30% actually bought the jam, nearly six times greater conversion rates. This is just one study of many that demonstrates that less is more – the more choices someone has, the less likely he or she is to make a decision.

How does this idea of having too many options impact conversion rates?

In the way you design your call to action. What I mean by a call to action is the next step you are asking your audience to take, such as place an order, call you for more information, or fill out a sign-up form.

If you increase the number of calls to action on your website, the less likely your audience will take a next step. Just with Iyengar and Lepper's jam experiment, the more choices someone has, the less likely they are to make a sale. As a starting point, only have one call to action above the fold.

Create a clear path, give them certainty, and tell them the one thing they need to do next in order to do business with you.

The sooner you remove the extra distractions for your customers, the sooner they will do business with you. Don't put them in a situation where they have to decide twice: first if they want to do business with you and second how they are going to contact you.

The way you design the next step you want your clients to take will have a massive impact on conversion rates. Great website design is not about adding things. It's about taking things away.

Limit the calls to action you have on your website, and you will see an increase in conversion rates.

Key Takeaway #11

Reducing the number of call to actions will increase the number of people that contact you.

THERE CAN BE ONLY ONE

The one really important design principle that will take you a long way to becoming a better designer and marketer – there can be only one.

There can be only one font.

There can be only one main color.

There can be only one main focus.

There can only be one amount of text spacing.

There can only be one call to action.

You should decide early on what your branding style guide is going to be and stick to it. Pick one font that you are going to use for all of your sales copy. Pick one main color for your logo and branding. The previous chapter about how colors impact conversion rates will be a great starting point for you to build a brand around.

Don't make the mistake of making your website look cluttered and messy with multiple fonts and areas of focus that only prompt the user to become confused and click away. Your audience is looking for certainty and a clear path forward. Remove the mental roadblocks from your website and marketing material by making it as clean and simple as possible.

Probably the most important actionable thing to remember is that you should never split the attention of the audience. You want to control where the audience places their focus and what you want them to focus on next.

One message. One image. One call to action.

Simply scaling down your design to a few simple

elements creates the space for the sales message to take center stage.

The best design layout for your website is the one that draws primary focus to the sales copy. Any time that the design of your website is so bold that it takes the viewer's attention away from the sales message, you will see a drop in conversion rates.

The design of your website enables the marketing message, not the other way around. Take a look at some of the most successful marketing campaigns that really make you take notice. Odds are, the layout and design of the page was simple with only a few elements on the page.

A great way to think about this is to imagine yourself at a dinner party with a large group of people. What often happens is that two or three conversations are happening at the same time. Now, imagine you are sitting in the middle of this table listening to three different conversations at once. Your attention is split, and you are not really giving anyone your full attention, which leaves you feeling overwhelmed. This is the same thing that happens to new customers that come to your website when they see too many things going on at once.

Remember to give your customers the gift of simplicity; they will thank you for it with their business.

Key Takeaway #12

Never split the attention of your audience. Give them one main focus.

DESIGNING WEBSITES FOR MOBILE DEVICES

Depending which industry you are in and the age group that you are targeting, the first impression your new customers will get from your website could very well be on mobile.

Even if you have a desktop-focused product that will be used in an office space, the chances are that the first touchpoint with your product will be on a mobile phone. Every year, numbers show an increase in traffic from mobile devices, even in industries that have traditionally focused on desktop traffic. In 2017 63% of all website traffic came from mobile phone, up from 57% in 2016.

A great example of this is the travel industry. Currently, the fastest growing travel sites are not websites at all, but in fact mobile apps. People are now very comfortable making large purchases on mobile devices, and this trend is only going to continue.

How does this increase in traffic from mobile devices impact the decisions we make when we design websites moving forward?

All websites we build moving forward should be "responsive websites", which means that the design and layout of the sites changes when the users view them on different screen sizes.

The good news is that most website builders or frameworks have responsive features built-in, so you don't have to worry about getting it wrong.

The important thing is that you understand responsive design at a high level, so when you are working with a web designer or developer, you know what to look for.

The two things to consider when making your website truly responsive is what type of grid system you want and how you are going to size the elements on the page as the page gets smaller or bigger.

A website grid is a structured way to organize the content of the website and the best way to control how each section is placed when the screen size changes. Think of it like building blocks that transform when the area you are building in changes.

Changing the size of the elements on the page when the screen size changes is extremely important. Sometimes it's best to remove objects or images all together on mobile due to the limited screen size you have to work with.

In fact, Google Chrome lets you preview how your website will look on different screen sizes. You can test this the same way you test what area in your site is above the fold. Right-click on any area of the page. Then click on inspect from the list of options. This will bring up a pop-up window at the bottom of the page. In the pop-up window on the top left-hand corner, click on the icon that looks like a mobile phone. The option is called a "toggle device toolbar."

Take the time to make sure your website looks just as good on mobile as it would on a desktop. When you do this you will see a night a day difference in the user behavior on your site. More importantly, you will greatly increase the chances that your first-time visitors will stick around and want to do business with you.

If in doubt, speak with your web designer or web developer. As soon as you mention this to them, they should know what you are talking about and be able to help you.

Part Three: Technology

HOW TECHNOLOGY IMPACTS CONVERSION RATES

The goal of this section of the book is not to teach you how to code or to transform you into a data scientist. The goal is to highlight the handful of things that you do need to learn in order for you see things that you did not see before.

One of the biggest misconceptions people make about marketing is that technology alone will increase the results. This is not true. Marketing and design have a much larger impact on increasing conversion rates than technology ever will. The main reason for this is that even though technology has changed, the human mind has largely stayed the same. That's why the same underlying marketing principles that worked on radio and print ads also worked on the first TV ads.

This chapter will walk you through the three ways that technology impact conversion rates: qualification, automation, and measurement. This will help you see things that you did not see before and empower you to make data-driven decisions with your marketing campaigns.

Key Takeaway #13

Technology enables the marketing message, not the other way round.

HOW TO PRE-QUALIFY CUSTOMERS

One of the most exciting things for a business owner is meeting someone that is the perfect fit for their product or service. Very little selling needs to take place. In fact, they are selling you on ways you can do business together. This is exciting because so much of traditional selling is about dealing with rejection and learning from the word "no".

Having someone that is ready and willing to buy is undoubtedly a great situation to be in, but how do we find these people, and better yet, how do we escape the feast-or-famine reality that plagues most small businesses and find these ideal buyers in a measurable and predictable way? So how do we find this audience of ideal clients each and every month?

By using advanced targeting.

What is advanced targeting?

Finding your ideal customer from any geographic location, any age group, any job title, or more. For instance, let's say you are a personal trainer in New York City who is focused on working with men and women over 50.

Now, if this was ten years ago you would have to rely on referrals or partnering with another company that already has contact with your ideal client. Don't get me wrong, referrals are great. They generally convert a very high level of accuracy because they are a warm introduction. However, the problem with referrals is that you are dependent on other sources for leads, thus making it is very hard to predict your outcome in each given month. It's difficult to scale when you have no idea how many new clients you will get next month.

Now, fast forward to today, and you can very easily get your marketing material in front of men and women over 50 living in New York City. All you need to do is take advantage of the audience targeting on social media platforms, such as Facebook, Instagram, or Twitter. Even YouTube ads have advanced targeting now. All major social media platforms are doing this and, best of all, the ads are actually cheaper than what you would spend on a print ad in a New York City newspaper.

What do you think would happen to your marketing results if you only advertised to people that fit your ideal client profile? You will spend less money and make more. You can do this — it's not rocket science. The reality is that today, some of the smartest minds in the world right now are not working to put a man into space or to cure cancer. They are finding new and better ways to sell products online.

You don't need a deep understanding of advertising to know how to use these targeting platforms. All you need to do is set a marketing budget. Define the audience of people you want to see your ad. In this example, it's men and women over 50 years of age living in New York City. Then create an ad using the marketing and design principles you have learnt in this book. All you need to do now is click "start campaign," and you are off and running.

The first time you do this. you will be shocked at how easy it is, and you will never, ever look at traditional print or radio ads the same way again. Just to be clear, I'm not one of those people who says print and radio ads are dead. I personally know people that have built very successful businesses using print and radio ads almost exclusively. People still read newspapers, and people still listen to the radio, so old-school tactics can still work.

The one thing I would say is this: a test campaign for print or radio normally requires you to commit to a large marketing budget upfront with few options to change the campaign when it is up and running. Now, this is okay if you are a master of marketing and know your audience like the back of your hand. However, if you are still figuring out who your ideal customer profile may be, it's a very expensive way to learn from your mistakes. It's like learning to play poker for the first time by sitting down at the high stakes table. You can do it, but it's going to be a very expensive lesson.

I recommend you start by spending your advertising dollars on digital ads only to begin with for one simple reason. You get the data almost instantly. Spending money on print and radio ads could take weeks before you know if your marketing dollars have been profitable or not. On the other hand, setting up a targeted ad campaign on Facebook could give you the answers you need in under 24 hours. This short feedback loop is how you can become a very strong and capable marketer in a very short period of time.

The advertising data is what you need. One piece of data is better than 100 expert opinions. Opinions are cheap and are often formed from a very small amount of data. Your path to becoming a better marketing starts with you embracing the mindset of making data-driven decisions.

We are now living in the golden age of targeted marketing. Never before has it been so easy to get in front of people that need your product or service at scale. Use this extreme targeting to your advantage.

Your specific product is best in the hands of a very specific person. This fact should be the lighthouse for every marketing decision you ever make. When you start targeting and stop blanketing your marketplace, your results will respond like you never thought possible.

THE FASTEST WAY TO GO BROKE WHEN SPENDING MONEY ON ADVERTISING

Before you spend a single dollar on advertising you need to clearly define what you can afford to spend to acquire a new customer. Skipping this important step is the fastest way to go broke when spending money on ads. I understand that you want to get started, and you are excited to see the results, but this important first step is what separates the winners from the losers.

Sit down and work out to the dollar what the average client is worth to you. Some of you may already be thinking, are we talking about the upfront value or the lifetime value? If you have enough data that can track the lifetime value of a client in dollars, then go with the lifetime value. For everyone else, play it safe and focus on the upfront value.

Personally, I always try to think about relationships with a long-term time frame, but sometimes that is not realistic. There are hard costs in running a business. If you find yourself in a situation where you are spending $48 to acquire a new customer, but this new customer is only making one purchase for $32, you are losing money every time you make a sale.

This happens all the time. Companies of all sizes spend more money to acquire a new client than that customer's worth to the business.

Part of the problem is that companies have recently started to solely focus on growth or brand awareness when it's profitability that keeps the lights on. This is terrible for the owners of the company that end up paying the bills at the end of the month.

That's why it always pays to look at what small businesses are doing to find new customers. They count every dollar in and out of their business and can't afford to spend money without achieving a positive result.

That's why when small businesses have to spend their own hard-earned money on advertising they never talk in terms of brand awareness. The only question they ask themselves is: for every dollar I spend on advertising, how much money do I expect to see back from that dollar? Turning advertising dollars into profit is the name of the game.

This formula of turning advertising dollars into profit starts with defining your break-even point in terms of what you can spend to find a new customer.

After you know how much you can spend to acquire a new customer you have taken the first major step in creating marketing reports that will give you a clear snapshot of the results of your marketing efforts.

The dollar amount you decide on will be measured against the total costs of your advertising efforts to determine if your marketing is profitable or not. This is the beginning of creating a marketing campaign that can scale with predictable results.

THE MATH THAT MAKES YOU MONEY

Now that you have defined what you can afford to spend to acquire a new customer, it's time to set up the marketing reports that will act as a scoreboard for your marketing results. You want to put yourself in a position from day one where you have all the data and information in one place, so you can make data-driven marketing decisions.

The crazy thing is that most people hate reporting. They think it's boring. If you think marketing reports are boring, you probably haven't run a successful marketing campaign before. For me personally, it is the most exciting part of my job. I am so hungry to increase conversion rates and lower advertising costs that I get obsessed with my reports.

Just to be clear, we must have all the marketing reports setup before we spend a single dollar on ads. We need all the data from day one. This information is critical to the long-term success of your marketing results. Chances are you may have already spent money on ads without the correct reporting. This is a great opportunity to go over the previous results of campaigns and use these numbers as a starting point for your marketing reports.

There are two main reasons why we use marketing reports like the one I am about to share with you.

They are the simplest way to track the return on investment from your marketing dollars, and they are the best early warning system for when things go wrong. This is very underrated and extremely important when the campaign starts to scale up.

The marketing reporting system we use to track our results is broken up into three sections. The exciting thing about breaking up the marketing reports into three section is that we get very granular and look at the smallest details related to how they could be impacting conversion rates. One of the benefits of this is that you turn your mindset away from only thinking about the end conversion rate and devote your focus to conversion events. It's all about tracking and improving on the small conversion events, such as how many seconds someone watched a video. These small wins stacked together are what generate massive increases in conversion rates.

1. Traffic Report

The traffic report details the performance metrics and costs of getting your marketing message in front of your target audience. This is the cost of engagement with a new customer. This is not just clicks or views. This is also how many people viewed the ad vs. how many people clicked on it. Also, it examines the position your ad on the page and other important ranking factors that act as benchmarks for how the ad is performing. All of this information is used to get a complete picture.

The key thing to remember about the traffic report is not about getting cheap clicks or views. It's about getting relevant clicks and views. We want traffic that has commercial intent — people with a high probability that they will want to do business with us. Reducing the cost per click is often a good thing, but sometimes it's better to pay a little bit more for traffic that you can actually make money from.

There is a lot of technical jargon around performance metrics, so don't stress out if you don't understand everything the first time around. The best way to get over this is to read the documentation on the ad platform you are using. It will explain all the key terms that relate to that ad network. The get started guide should answer most of your questions, and the rest you will learn as you go along.

2. Website/Landing Page Report

The landing page report is all about what happens after the user clicks on your ad. This report focuses on user behavior. Good news is that since the user is now on your site, we have complete control over the user experience.

This is where we start tracking website conversion rate events. This can be submitting a form, placing an order, or calling to book an appointment. Any time a user completes a call to action, we need to track it and turn it into a metric.

The next step in this report is to take our new conversion rate data and compare that with the information in the traffic report to see how much money we have spent for that conversion to take place. This is how we define website cost metrics. An example of this would be cost per add to cart or cost per new subscriber. Putting together cost metrics is the best way to assign a dollar amount on every action that happens on your website.

When you start linking user behavior to cost metrics, everything that the user does on your site becomes more meaningful. This is where we get to take advantage of all the new marketing principles we have learnt.

3. Operations Report
The operations report focuses on what happens after a user has done something. The keyword here is "something". Yes, this does include sales and new conversions, but it also includes incomplete orders or drop-off points. Fixing leaks in this area of your website often produces the largest results out of any other changes.

Fixing problems in this area is often a mixture of technical and customer service improvements. The customer completed 90% of the process but left the site for some reason. It is your job to find out what that reason is, and this report helps you do that. The data in this report is often a great starting point to speak with people that didn't become a customer for some reason and fix those leaks so that it will not happen again. I learnt very early on that the market and your customers are always right. Listen to them.

With these three reports now in hand, you have all the information you need to make data-driven decisions with your marketing campaigns. Learn to love these three marketing reports, and they will give you all the information you need to make better decisions with your website.

FREE TOOLS THAT ARE WORTH MILLIONS

One of the most exciting things about marketing in the digital age is that much of the heavy lifting is already done for us. Data collection and data comparison are now automatically done in the background, so we can just focus on the end results.

By now you are probably wondering what marketing software I use to conduct my split tests. There are many different online tools that help you track the results of marketing experiments. I have used all of the major ones and, to be honest, they all do roughly the same thing with small differences in user experience and cross-platform integration. After using many different types of split testing tools, I now have a very clear idea of what features I need and what is just a useless add-on that doesn't make judging the results of split tests any easier.

At their core, split testing tools have two main functions: recording the conversion rate results of two different versions of the same website and taking that data and using a mathematical formula called statistical significance to declare a winner with mathematical certainty.

You don't need to understand any mathematical formulas to use these split testing tools. In fact, they are designed in a way that you don't have to do any calculations whatsoever. All you need to understand is this: the data declares the winner, not you. One great leap forward for you as a marketer is putting your own opinions to the side and graduating to the mindset of making only data-driven decisions.

With that being said, out of all the split testing tools that I have used, which one would I recommend to you? In my experience, the best split testing tool is Google Optimize. There are four main reasons that I think Google Optimize is the best choice when deciding on a split testing tool.

1. It has the simplest and most robust integration with Google Analytics.
2. The software is completely free, with no upfront costs and no subscription costs.
3. The user experience is simple and gives you all the information you need.
4. Anyone can use it, You don't need to know how to write code or hire a web developer.

When Google Optimize hit the market, it was a complete game changer. Up to that point, we had three or four different software providers, all charging over $100 per month for what Google

Optimize is now offering for free. One really important point to remember is that the best part about Google Optimize is not that it's free. The best part is that it directly integrates with Google Analytics. Now we have all the data for paid traffic, organic traffic, and split testing results all in one place. This gives you the freedom to automatically create reports with a complete overview of what is going on with your website.

Google Optimize is without a doubt the best split testing software I have ever used. Even though this is a free product, I have personally used it to manage multi-million dollar advertising campaigns. It has all of the features you need to conduct a successful split test no matter how much traffic you have coming to your page. Stop paying for expensive marketing software that you don't need. Use Google Optimize, and you will be glad you did.

HOW WEBSITE PERFORMANCE IMPACTS CONVERSION RATES

One technical factor that you need to understand very early on is that website performance matters. What I mean by that is how fast your website loads has a direct impact on your customers and your conversion rates. If they have to wait for longer than three seconds, you are giving them a reason to leave. I see this problem all the time.

I understand that you want to create a fancy website with images and animations, but this can have a negative impact on your customers and your business.

To check if our website is running slow or not, you can use Google's free page speed tool. All you need to do is type in your URL and, within a few seconds, Google will bring back a detailed report on how quickly your page loads. Simply search for "google page speed test," and it will be the first page result.

The results of this page speed report from Google are going to be different for every site, but here are some problems that I often see when running page speed tests. Some of these factors you will have to speak to a web developer about, but it's important that you know what they are when speaking with the person that is building your site.

1. Reduce the file size of the images you have on your site. Make the file size as small as you can while still keeping the image quality.

2. Reduce the amount of JavaScript you have to load on each page of your site. You will probably have to speak to your web developer about this one, but reducing the amount of code you have to load will have a very positive impact on the speed of your site.

3. Combine your CSS files into one file if you can, so the server does not have to load multiple CSS files. Again speak to your web developer about this.

4. If you have a high-traffic site, it might be a good idea to upgrade your hosting service to a dedicated server instead of a shared server. Sharing server resources with thousands of other websites will reduce the cost of your hosting but will also limit the amount of data you can send at any given time.

5. Host video content with an external provider. Hosting video content on your own server is only going to cause you problems. Companies like YouTube and Vimeo have made it very easy for

people to upload video content that loads in seconds. They have hosting video content all figured out, so there is no reason to go out and do it on your own.

6. Reduce the number of plugins and other tracking software you have on your site. Think very carefully about adding extra plugins that need to load before the page does. This can cause large increases in page load times.

7. Reduce site redirects. This means that two web pages need to be loaded before the user can see the information that they are looking for.

8. Track mobile and desktop load times as two separate things. Aim to create a slimmed-down version of your site that is designed for mobile users with slow or limited data plans.

9. Last but not least, track page speed over time. The way websites are being loaded changes all the time, so you should check in regularly to see how your site is performing.

Well, that is a high-level overview of how website performance impacts conversion rates. I highly recommend you run the speed test yourself, so you can get an idea of what is going on. Then speak with your web developer to get the website code problems all fixed up.

THE ONLY LONG-TERM GOAL THAT MATTERS

When running advertising campaigns, it's easy to get emotional about the results. Some of the split tests you run are going to win, and some are going to lose. You have to learn to mentally deal with the swings.

What is the long-term goal of running split tests? Increase conversion rates? Yes, but that is just the beginning. Our long-term goal is much bigger and more important than that.

Our long-term goal with running split tests and marketing campaigns in general is to easily and predictably multiply money. What do I mean by that?

We want to be at a stage where we can predict with a high level of certainty what we can expect to get back in return for every dollar we spend. This is the only long-term goal that matters.

So much of marketing and advertising is uncertainty, and if we can escape from that and get to a place where we know to the dollar what our return on investment will be, all of our business stress and worries will melt away.

Marketing, when done right, should never be seen as an expense; it should always be seen as an investment that brings in a return. This shift in mindset will give you the peace of mind of knowing that whatever happens next month, as long as you spend money on advertising, you will be okay.

Think long term. We are in the game to turn advertising dollars into profit. Everything else is secondary. When you get to the point where you can predictably turn advertising dollars into profit each and every month, you have now won the game.

Bringing it All Together

HOW TO CREATE YOUR FIRST SPLIT TEST

By now you must be so excited to start making changes to your website and launch your first split test. I'm glad you are so excited. Let me walk you through the steps of what you should focus on first, so you have the best chance of booking your first split testing win.

The first thing you should change that will have the biggest impact is testing a new headline above the fold on your homepage or the page of your site that you are trying to make changes to.

Without even knowing what your business or

product is and taking what we have learnt from this book, we would make a new headline that focuses on the following key factors:

We borrow from the timeless wisdom of Sun Tzu and gather all the information we possibly can about our audience. This gives us the strategic advantage of knowing everything there is to know about who our audience is, so we can create a new headline that speaks directly to them.

Gone are the days where we target everyone. We have one person in mind, and that is the only person we want to target.

We would make sure that the new headline uses the immense power of the Napoleon rule by only focusing on your audience's self-interest. This means selling benefits not features. Remember, they don't care about you or your product. They only care about what you can do for them.

We would then make the headline as specific as we

possibly can. Now that you know that nothing turns customers away faster than a vague promise, learn from this and take action. People do not make a buying decision based on general information. The more details you give, the more dollars you get.

We would also make sure we only have one simple call to action. Reducing the number of calls to action is a separate split test unto itself, but this one is a no-brainer and an easy early win for us.

Lastly, we will start the split test using Google Optimize and let the test run until it achieves statistical significance.

Follow these steps and you have booked your first win and increased the conversion rates of your website.

I would love to hear about your success and how the principles in the book have made a positive impact on your business. Feel free to contact me on my website to share your story.

I am cheering for you.

FINAL THOUGHTS

By now, I hope you share my excitement for increasing conversion rates. Running split tests and booking massive wins is incredibly satisfying and very addictive. Discovering the principles in this book has changed my life and the way I look at marketing and business in general. I hope they will do the same for you.

Above all else, I hope this book has helped you to put yourself in a position where you can spend money on advertising and turn that money into profit.

NEED MORE HELP OR HAVE QUESTIONS?

I hope this book has helped you. If you need more help or have any questions about what was discussed in this book, feel free to contact me through my website www.joshpanebianco.com. I will get back to you as soon as I can. Thank you!

THANK YOU